The Quick Recipe Book

My Magical Cottage Core Life

The Quick Recipe Book

My Magical Cottage Core Life

(Hey, this part matters, so please read it.)

First Printing, 2023

Second Printing, 2024

Revised Edition for Spiral Moon Media, 2024

Spiral Moon Media Edition

Published by Spiral Moon Circle Publishing

Troy MI

2024

ISBN 978-0-9914926-1-9

Hi there!

I wanted to start our third year with a tasty offering. Recipes are a way to share time, space, and love with each other. This little book will be the first of a series companions to the show.

I hope they bring you joy and sustenance. Don't be shy to change them to suit your family. Or don't. I'm not the boss of you.

The recipes are not divided by type, so that you can randomly turn to a page and discover them. They are also quick.

There are spaces everywhere for notes.

Let's get started.

Apricot Treat

- 1 can Apricots, halved
- 1 can sweetened condensed milk

A simple recipe for hectic times. This dish is easy to make in the kitchen on the stovetop, or at an outing on a hot plate.

Drain the apricots. Add to a small pot. Pour in the milk. Now, very slowly warm over a low fire. Be watchful so that the milk does not scorch. Serve in small dishes or cups.

The thing I love about apricots is that they are so cute. Fuzzy little fruits with cute little cheeks. It makes you want to squeeze them. Like, all the time.

One of my fondest memories from working in Head Start was garden season. Every year, my delight was giving the parents, and teachers, seeds and plants. Apricots were on my list of trees to try next.

But, life happens. The wanderings of our hearts lead us to new places, new friends, and new times. I sometimes see the little faces, now grown large, in the community gardens in Detroit.

Those hands that were planting lima beans in paper cups are raising raspberry brambles. They enjoy a wider variety of fruits and vegetables than many other children. They also have a healthy attitude toward where food comes into their world.

Apricots also have another use. You can use the skins to make a dye. I am not going to ruin the surprise by telling you what color they make. This is a fun activity you can share with others, or your own awesome self.

This dye is cute for tea towels, aprons, and napkins. It will make any kitchen have a touch of homespun charm. Just keep in mind to add plenty of salt.

One word of caution. Apricots will make you very regular in your bathroom visits. That is to say, they are a natural ease on your digestive system, if you catch my hint.

Do you have a favorite apricot memory?

Simple Supper

- 1-2 lbs dry beans, red or kidney
- Tiger Teeth or Cayenne peppers
- 1 tsp dried lovage leaves, (optional)
- 2 chopped shallots
- 1 cup brown sugar

Wash and soak beans overnight. Wash again. Sort and discard any stones or bad beans. Add shallots. Chop and add peppers whole. Cook for up to 120 minutes, or until done if you substitute a larger bean.
During the last 30 minutes of cooking, add sugar and lovage.

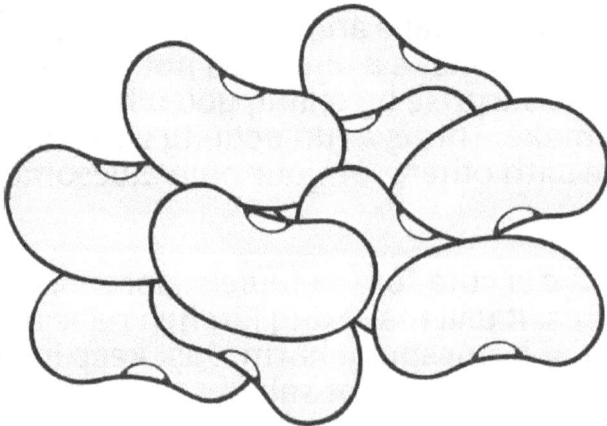

I see you looking at that recipe for beans in the simple supper. I know exactly, I think, which item made you pause. It was the Tiger Teeth peppers, right?

Those are some tasty little nuggets of pepper goodness. But, they are not always easy to find. I get it.

So, what does one do when the item is unavailable?

Well, you could try the local plant and garden exchanges. The internet is awesome for connecting people. There might be a gardener with a stash.

OR you could go online and buy them. There is always that option.

Just remember to check in your area for your planting times. That last frost date is not in any way a joke. Especially in Michigan. But my favorite thing to do is experiment with what I have. Using what is in your pantry, or your market, is always best. Cooking should be fun.

While the treasure hunt for peppers is tempting, it is not always practical. The dish will be just fine without them. I promise.

What is your favorite pepper?

Starry Night Grapes

1/2 cup cane or raw sugar
3 lbs concord grapes
1 tbsp white sparkling sugar

Snip all grapes into 3 grape bunches. Wash and swirl in clean water.

Add to a large punchbowl. Using a light touch, gently toss grapes and sugar. Dust with sparkling sugar once settled. Serve cold.

So, let's talk about grapes.

While they are tasty and sweet, I will tell you a secret. They are not just for sugary treats. Not at all.

In many kitchens in Michigan, they are spiced. That's right. They are pickled, or prepared with pepper. Let's go letter "P" for the win.

Jarring them with grains of paradise, or Szechuan peppercorns, and thyme, will give you a delightful flavor. You can find recipes on this. Turkish cooking is famous for these.

Here in the Mitten, we are blessed by exposure to so many cultural dishes. As children, it's almost impossible to not taste at least 9 different sorts of ethnic food before age 5.

I was in my teens when I was taught to peel grapes. Don't judge me. It was a pesticide awareness thing.

They taste kinda good that way. But I like the pop of the skins. Those skins also make a lovely dye.

Grape vines are all over the place here. Add a little bit of time and patience, and they turn into a lovely drink. You can add that juice to red sumac lemonade.

What is your favorite grape recipe?

The Pleasant Punch

2 liters Vernor's Ginger Ale soda
1 quart apple juice
3 sticks cinnamon
5 Red Hot Candies

This is a make ahead drink.

In a fairly large pot, slowly warm the apple juice. Add the candies and cinnamon sticks just as it begins to bubble. Add the Vernor's to the blend, and let cool. Add 2 cups of ice before serving.

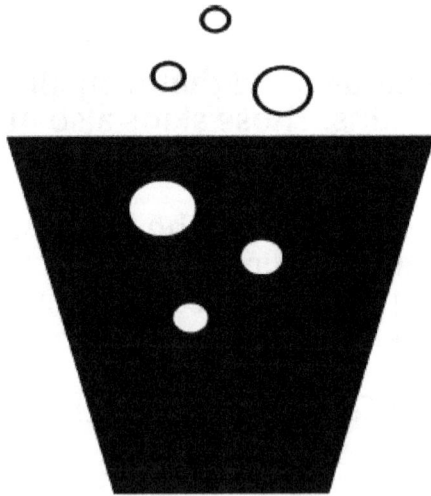

I prefer Vernor's ginger ale. I typed out soda for the recipe. It hurt me deep inside my soul. Here, we call it pop.

We use it for cold relief. A couple liters, and some orange juice, make a stay at home day with the sniffles bearable. Of course, we are absolutely convinced of its legendary curative abilities.

Don't argue facts with a Michigander.

We usually add Vick's Vaporub to the rite. A bit of that on the feet and chest is the regular practice. If we are really sick, we add it to the vaporizer.

Vernor's also gets used in church punch. Like, a LOT. Children pretend they are drinking some sort of children friendly beer. Hmmm, we might want to look at that later.

Another thing you can add to this is actual ginger, and heat up a pot of the ale. It's so powerful. It tastes so good.

Finally, you can bake cakes with it. A can, to a box of mix, and some pumpkin pie spice. Yum. Yes, pumpkin spice is really a thing here.

Have you ever had Vernor's? What do you make with it?

Corned Popovers

1 lb corned beef from deli, sliced to preference
¾ lb sliced baby swiss cheese
1 box cream cheese, softened
½ cups whole milk or half and half
2 pkgs crescent rolls, or make your own (I am not the boss of you)
Dill Seeds
½ stick Butter

In a skillet, melt butter on low. Heat corned beef just enough to sear the slices. Remove from heat.

Mix milk, cream cheese, and dill seeds. Set aside.

In a buttered casserole dish, lay a layer of crescent rolls. Add milk and cheese mixture. Layer in half the corned beef. Add ½ of cheese slices. Repeat. Top with the final layer of cheese. Bake at 350 degrees F til bubbly and golden on edges.

Let cool for 10 minutes. Slice into portions and serve.

I love corned beef. I grew up eating it. The smell brings back so many memories.

I can not eat as much now. It is not the salt content. I cannot process pork in my body. You read that right. Some lunch meat counters carry tubes of it with pork mixed into it.

But a good corned beef dish is a thing of beauty.

I remember my Mama brought home sandwiches some days. They would have Russian dressing, or Thousand Island, and were so good. I would pick the slaw from it, though.

As my palate matured, I stopped picking off the kraut and slaw. It really depends on my mood, though. The versatility of it is perfect for my moods.

Did you know you can also make a really good cold tortilla with it? Just roll it up, with a pickle in the center. I like Kosher dills, but Polish dills work well.

A good sandwich of corned beef, a side of pickled herring, and some Vernor's is a good time.

Do you have a favorite corned beef recipe?

Sausage and Apples

2 - 5 lbs Smoked sausage of your choice
1 small head of cabbage, shredded
5 apples, quartered, peeled
¼ cup apple cider vinegar
½ apple juice
1 cup Chicken Stock or Vegetable stock
1 sliced onion or half a jar of pearl onions

Cut sausages into 3 inch lengths. Place in a slow cooker or into a Dutch oven. Add apples and rest of the ingredients. Cook low for 4 hours OR on low til cabbage is translucent. Enjoy.

Who doesn't love a good sausage, if you eat meat?

Making sausage is a really messy job. But you can take shortcuts. You don't have to set up a giant black iron cook pot in the yard.

Run, Babe, Run!!!

Buy some sausage seasoning and add it to your own meat blend. You can make it free form into patties to avoid the casing. Frying it up for breakfast is a dream.

Keep in mind that making sausage comes with specific instructions. If you are not keeping it frozen, follow them to the letter. When you make your own, you control what you put into your mouth. We've chatted about this on the podcast. Don't just put anything into your mouth. Know what it is.

You can substitute pears for apples in that recipe. The taste will be different, but it will work. If you are adventurous, try some pink lady apples.

Have you ever had a pink lady apple?

Lemon Splurge

1 can lemon pie filling
1 container Cool Whip
2 1 qt packages of strawberries, rinsed and sliced

In a plastic bowl, whip together the pie filling and Cool Whip. Using a spatula, spoon into a clear serving dish. Place strawberry slices in a fish scale pattern all over the top. Serve cold.

Bites for Little Sprites

This is an easy snack for small hands to handle.

1 bag of apples, sliced in half horizontally, and cored, and washed
1 container feta cheese
Honey, or agave syrup, depending on preference.
1 package dried dates, chopped

Mix the honey and goat cheese together in a small bowl. Add dates. Spread between apple halves and serve to the hungry littles at the gathering.

Two recipes for little people. That was fun.

There is enough room for your notes, as always. But if you try, you can also let a little person color on that page. Maybe they can make a fingerprint. That way, you can write their age next to it.

I'm a Mom, what do you want from me?

Having tiny hands in the kitchen gives them life learning. Knowing where the food grows, cooks, and preps fosters kindness and gratitude. Kindness is a skill, like many graces.

Learning how to set a place is also a skill that goes here.

Eating at fast food places is sometimes the only option many parents may have at family dining together. At least on a regular basis. But that doesn't mean that grace cannot be said, thanks given, and time taken.

The simple act of unfolding two napkins can make a world of difference. Making one a placemat can foster the habit of mindfulness. The other in the lap teaches care of clothing and belongings. It also shows care of appearance. All of these help self image.

Patience in the kitchen when cooking with little ones. They are learning to use their grip and fingers. Growing at such a fast pace means they are not always able to judge their abilities accurately.

Using fruits and veggies to help with manipulative experiences is awesome.

What was your very first dish you cooked as a child?

Black Moon Grove Vegan Salad

1 3 lb bag of chopped broccoli, raw and
washed
1 box sultanas
Balsamic Vinegar
1 Bag of sunflower seeds

In a large dish, combine all ingredients. Add
vinegar according to taste. Serve.

*You can add spice berries to this.

Kyle's Hunter's Moon Cold Plate

On a platter board, assemble the following.

Summer sausage, sliced
Smoked Salmon, sliced
Roast beef, sliced (sensing a theme here?)
Roast turkey, sliced
Pepper Jack cheese
Cheddar
Port Salut
Smoked Gouda
Pemmican
Blueberries
Garlic Olives
Dried Plums
Dried Apricots
Dried Apples
Saltines
Salted Biscuits
Toasted Almonds
Walnuts
Pecans
Jalapenos (that's my Hubby)
Pumpernickel, Rye, Sourdough, and Flax
seed breads

Condiments are to your preference.

Garden in Spring Sandwiches

2 cups Pansy flowers
1 container whipped cream cheese
½ cup chopped burnet
1 Tbsp clover honey

Bread, encrusted and sliced into planks (feed the birds the crusts) Whip together the honey, burnet and cream cheese. Spread thinly on bread. Layer with flowers. Serve with an additional side of honey and a nice tea.

****
****
****
****

Check your flower seed stash. Germination testing is important.

Granvill E. Nesbitt's famous sardines and eggs.

You read that right.

1 can sardines in oil
2 eggs

In a bowl, mash sardines. Add eggs and blend. In a warm skillet, add butter and scramble the egg and fish mixture until cooked.

Mary H. Nesbitt's pork chops

4 - 6 pork chops
1 bowl of flour for dredging
GEL or Lawry's Seasoned salt
MSG
Corn oil

Wash your meat. Then season both sides, and dredge in flour. Fry til fat is golden, flipping twice during cooking. Flour should be crackling and dark amber. Marrow on bones should be cooked until no longer bleeding. Fat should be cooked well.

Brenna's Pasta Power Dish

1 box fettuccine
1 jar Alfredo sauce
2 lbs cooked, detailed shrimp, thawed
Salt for pasta water
2 Tbsp Italian Seasoning blend
Fresh cracked pepper
Red Pepper flakes
3 crushed cloves garlic

Cook noodles according to directions.

Drain.

Warm sauce in the pan.

Meanwhile, talk on a cell phone speaker while washing shrimp. Roll eyes at mother, and then saute the shrimp in butter, garlic, pepper and red pepper flakes. Fold in noodles, and then add to the pot of sauce. Add seasonings. Serve with garlic bread.

Kenya and Kyle Coviak's Hotter Jambalaya

1 lb ground beef
1 lb smoked sausage, sliced
1 can cream of chicken soup
1 can French Onion Soup
¾ cup rice
2 Tsp Kitchen Bouquet
1 small onion, chopped
3 ribs celery, chopped
1 bell pepper, chopped
2 Thai hot peppers

In a large pot (you will need one that you can cover later), sweat the vegetables until just translucent. Add sausage and caramelize. Add ground beef, and brown. Drain.

Add soups, Kitchen Bouquet, rice, and peppers. If it looks horrid, you are doing a great job, Sweetie.

(Yes, we know it is not made from scratch, so what? *cackles*)

Bake in the oven at 350 degrees F for 40 minutes, or until rice is done. It really depends on the oven and the humidity that day. If you cannot take heat, leave out the peppers.

I like adding ramps. Ramps are also known as bear garlic. If you can find it in spring, do it. Or buy at a farmer's market.

Squash Fritters

1 yellow crookneck squash, washed and cubed
½ cup cornstarch
½ tsp salt
Vegetable oil
Mix salt and cornstarch.

In a medium bowl, toss squash cubes in cornstarch. Let sit for 5 minutes. Toss again. It should feel a bit tacky.

In a large skillet, add enough oil to a depth of ½ inch minimum.

Now, heat over a medium flame.

Fry cubes, turning to avoid burning. Let them get golden.

Remove from heat and drain on paper.

Serve right away.

Summer Sanwiches

1 loaf pumpernickel bread, cut into discs
with a glass
1 block cream cheese
1 cup raspberries, washed
1 apple, peeled and minced
¼ cup blueberries, washed
½ tsp salt

In a small bowl, crush all berries.

Mix in the cream cheese, thoroughly
incorporating the berries.

Add the apple bits and salt.

Spread into the bread.

Serve with cold tea.

YOUR OTHER RECIPE NOTES

Thank you for taking this journey together.

I hope you find use in this humble little book. May it light the candle of creativity at your table, fill your cup with hopefulness, and fill your plate with potential. I wish your life's table to be abundant with blessings.

Finding recipes by just closing your eyes and opening the book was out of the ordinary. Right? Good.

It is good to do the unexpected. Keeps life interesting.

I love sharing things with my friends, and we're friends, right?

I also look forward to sharing some time with you on the podcast and in the social media groups. Small places can hold big feelings.

So til next time I take up my pen, I will meet you in the airways on the My Magical Cottagecore Life Podcast on Spotify.

Recipe Notes

Recipe Notes

Recipe Notes

www.ingramcontent.com/pod-product-compliance
Lightning Source LLC
Chambersburg PA
CBHW060211070426
42447CB00035B/3154